A FATHER'S MEMORY JOURNAL

Look back · Record · Treasure forever

Hardie Grant

QUADRILLE

THIS FATHER'S MEMORY
JOURNAL IS A GIFT TO

—————————————————

WITH LOVE FROM

—————————————————

Given name at birth

Date of birth

Place of birth

Relationship / marriage

Children

YOUR YOUTH

Your grandparents' names

Your grandparents' dates of birth

Where were your grandparents born?

What were your grandparents' occupations?

What did you enjoy most about your grandparents' company?

What memories did your grandparents share with you from their childhood?

Have you inherited any precious family keepsakes?

Do you, or I, resemble any of our ancestors?

Your mother's name

Your mother's date of birth

Your mother's place of birth

Your mother's occupation

Your father's name

Your father's date of birth

Your father's place of birth

Your father's occupation

How did your parents meet?

What's your earliest memory of your mother and father?

Did your parents have a happy marriage?

What did you admire about your parents?

Who were the members of your immediate family?

Names of your siblings

Your family pets?

What was your favourite toy?

Where did you like playing in your house?

Which books or television programmes made a big impact on you?

Did your parents introduce religion to you?

What was your favourite meal / treat?

How much pocket money did you receive?

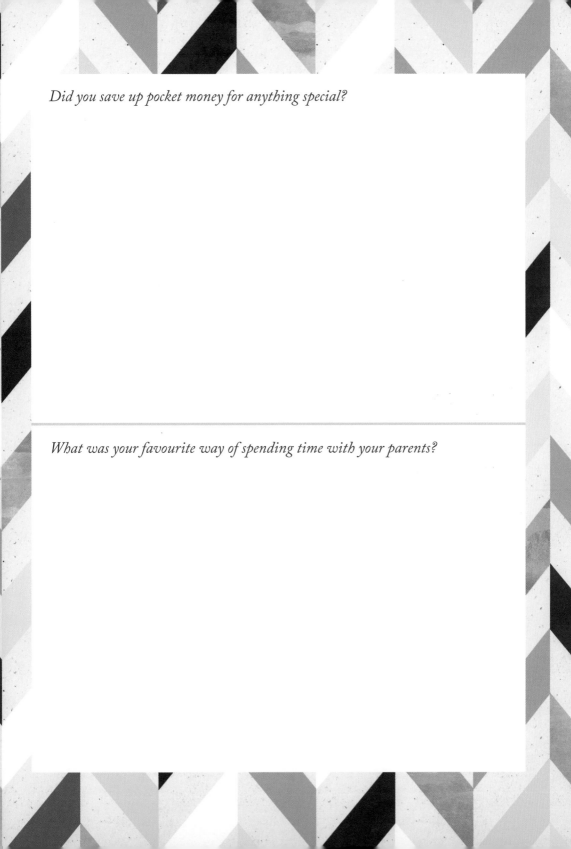

Did you save up pocket money for anything special?

What was your favourite way of spending time with your parents?

When were you happiest as a child?

What made you cry?

What was your favourite holiday as a child?

Who were your closest friends growing up?

Describe the most exciting games and activities you enjoyed playing as a child

How much time did you spend outside without adult supervision?

Did you organise any secret societies or clubs?

Were you ever in danger as a child?

What was the bravest thing you did as a child?

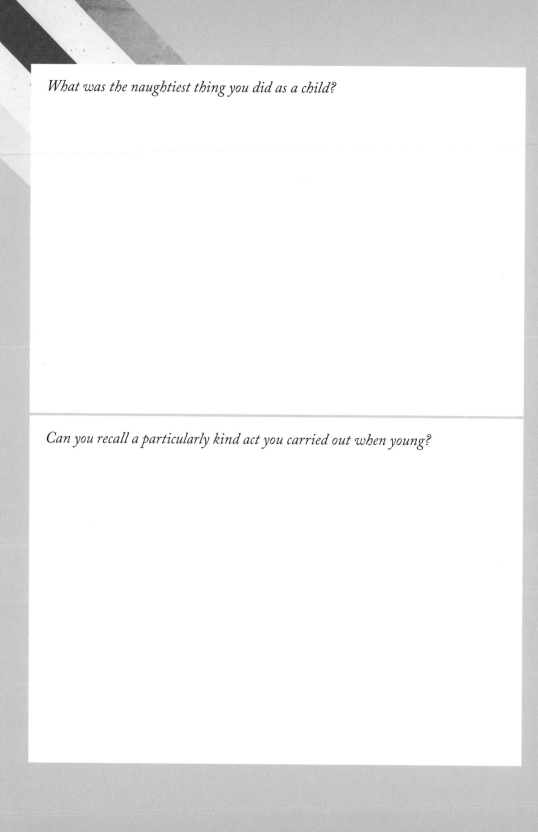

What was the naughtiest thing you did as a child?

Can you recall a particularly kind act you carried out when young?

What's the biggest obstacle you overcame when young?

Did you find anything particularly fascinating when you were growing up?

What's the first piece of news you remember hearing as a child?

Where did you go to school?

What were your favourite subjects at school?

Which subjects did you not enjoy?

Did your parents or teachers employ any punishments?

What was the most stupid thing you got up to in the classroom?

Were you a diligent or disruptive pupil?

Did any teachers inspire you?

Which qualifications did you achieve?

Who was your best friend?

Do you have any advice about how to avoid a fight or confrontation?

Did you play in any sports teams?

What was the first live match / sporting event you can remember watching?

Did you play a musical instrument, sing in a choir or act in a play?

Do you consider yourself creative?

What was the first record / CD / song you remember buying?

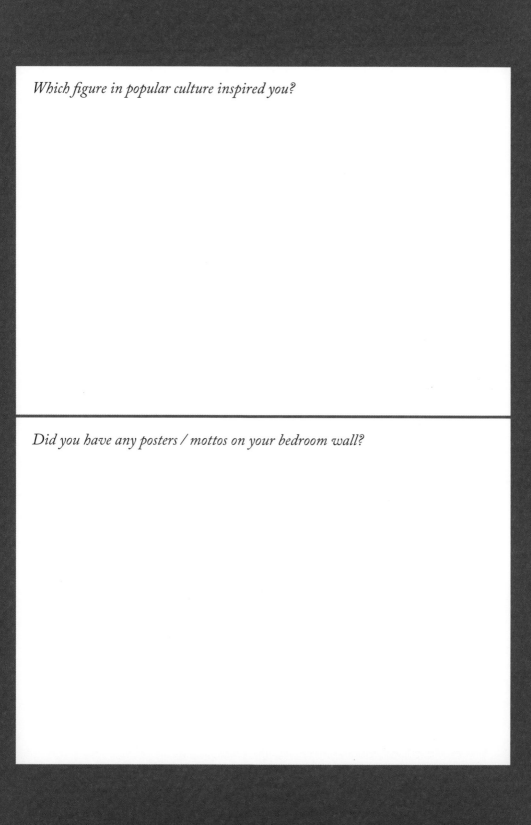

Which figure in popular culture inspired you?

Did you have any posters / mottos on your bedroom wall?

What newspapers or magazines were read in the family home?

What did you get up to during an ordinary weekend?

Can you remember any item of clothing that you particularly loved or loathed?

Is there a special meal that reminds you of your childhood?

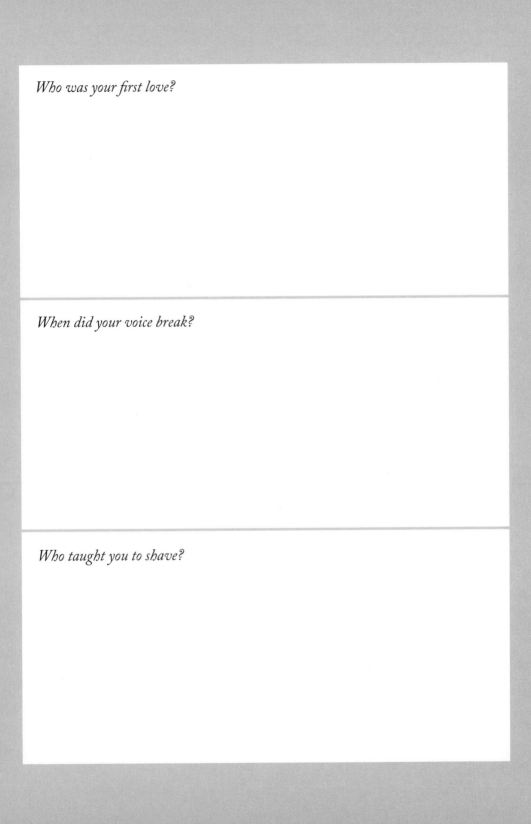

Who was your first love?

When did your voice break?

Who taught you to shave?

Did either parent teach you the "facts of life"?

When did you feel like a grown up?

ON BECOMING
A MAN

When did you start to care about your appearance?

Where was your first job?

How much did you earn?

When did you learn to drive?

What was your first car or bike?

What other vehicles have you driven?

What was your worst job?

When you first started going out, what was your idea of a good time?

Are there any venues that hold particularly special memories?

Where and with whom was your first date?

Did you have many girlfriends?

When did you leave home?

What further education / training did you undertake?

When did you become financially independent?

What piece of advice would you pass to your 21-year-old self?

How did you know what you wanted to be when you grew up?

When was the first time you got a job / set up a business you were really proud of?

A family tree is a diagram which charts the relationships of each generation within a family. The branches of the tree connect each person to their parents, spouses and children.

You can start with the oldest generation at the top and the newer generations at the bottom. You can make it more complete by adding branches for cousins, aunts and uncles, or keep it focused and create a family tree with only parents, grandparents and siblings – it can be as simple or as complex as you like. For extra detail, you can record both maiden and married names, as well as dates of births and deaths.

FAM
TR

ILY

EE

Which aspect of your working life has made you most proud?

For which achievements within your career would you like to be remembered?

Any advice about dealing with annoying colleagues?

How has your career differed from that of your parents'?

What has motivated you to progress in your career?

What's the best investment you've made?

Do you have any investment advice for me?

Have you been involved with any political causes?

What makes you laugh?

Can you describe your sense of humour?

What's your idea of a perfect weekend?

Did you ever do anything as a young man that you find completely embarrassing now?

What's your advice on maintaining good friendships?

How do you deal with criticism?

Where did you and my mother meet?

What first attracted you to my mother?

Where did you and my mother go on your first date?

What made you decide to propose / stay together?

Were your parents and my mother's parents supportive of your relationship?

Share any secrets you've discovered about sustaining a happy relationship

STARTING
A FAMILY

Names of your children

Dates of birth of your children

Where were they born?

Were there any children that are no longer here?

Did you plan to have a family?

Can you remember what you thought when my mother said she was pregnant?

How nervous were you as the birth approached?

Describe the journey to and from the hospital

What can you remember most vividly about the day I was born?

How did your feelings to my mother evolve after I was born?

Who chose my name? What does it mean to you?

Describe how you felt holding me for the first time

BRINGING ME UP

Record any memorable incidents that occurred
when you looked after me as a baby

How much did you help my mother with the
nappy changing and sleepless nights?

Was there a particular method, routine or song you used to get me to sleep?

Which elements of the baby years did you really enjoy?

Which elements of the baby years did you struggle with?

What games did you play with me when I was a child?

Which part of our daily routine did you most enjoy?

Can you describe a special day that you and I spent together?

Describe our first holiday as a young family

Can you describe any mannerisms or funny characteristics I had when I was younger?

Did the family dynamics change as your family grew?

Did stress ever become a serious issue?

What strategies did you use to keep going?

Can you share any tips for managing work and family life balance?

What was your preferred method for relaxing?

When were you most worried on my behalf?

Can you describe the love you feel for me?

What are the highlights and lowlights about having a teenage child?

What did you think about my first relationship?

What was our worst row about?

What did you think about my friends?

Do you see your younger self in me?

What was your main hope for me as I grew into an adult?

What are some of your proudest moments as a father?

BEING A FATHER, BEING YOU

What event has had the biggest impact on your life?

What's the greatest compliment you've ever received?

What was your relationship like with your father?

What do you think are the most important skills for a father to possess?

If your house was on fire, which object would you want to save?

What similarities do I share with you?

What do you think you got right as a father?

What could you have done differently as a father?

Which aspect of fatherhood has given you the most pleasure?

What would you like to be remembered for?

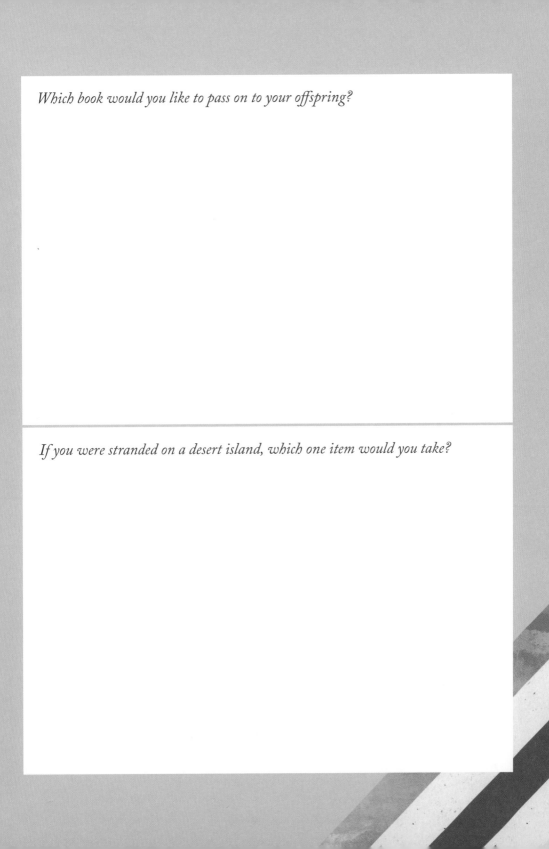

Which book would you like to pass on to your offspring?

If you were stranded on a desert island, which one item would you take?

What more do you want to achieve in life?

When was the happiest time of your life?

When was the saddest time of your life?

What do you think has been the greatest invention in your lifetime?

How has the idea of being a man changed in your lifetime?

Describe a moment in history that you will never forget

Record the most valuable piece of advice you have been given

Is there a physical or inherited trait unique to our family?

Are there any family health issues we should discuss?

Is there a family secret still not told?

Which family traditions would you like us to continue?

Record family quotes that have passed down the generations

Describe a famous family anecdote

What is your most precious wish for future generations of our family?

How do you think the world could improve in the next 10 years?

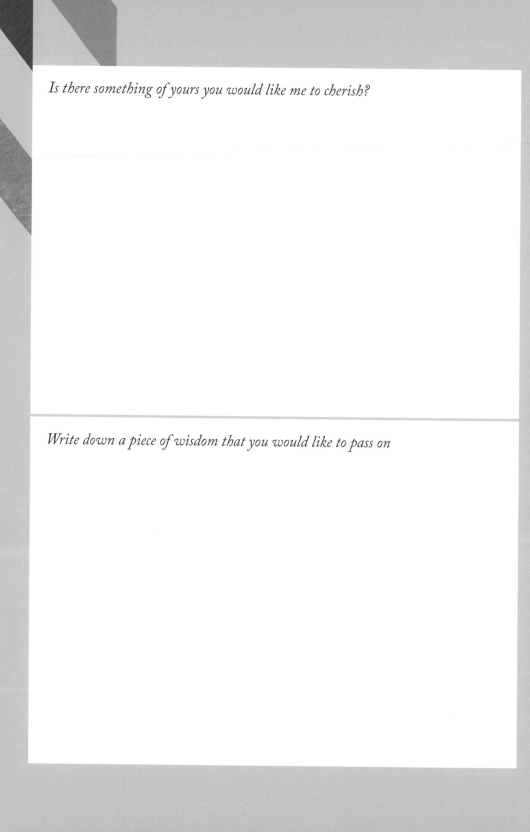

Is there something of yours you would like me to cherish?

Write down a piece of wisdom that you would like to pass on

BUSINESS DEVELOPMENT DIRECTOR Melanie Gray

ASSISTANT EDITOR Stacey Cleworth

AUTHOR Joanna Gray

DESIGNERS Katherine Keeble and Gemma Hayden

PRODUCTION DIRECTOR Vincent Smith

PRODUCTION CONTROLLER Sinead Hering

Published in 2019 by Quadrille,
an imprint of Hardie Grant Publishing

Quadrille
52–54 Southwark Street
London SE1 1UN
quadrille.com

ISBN 978 1 78713 496 6

Printed in China